Snow Poems

Compiled by John Foster

OXFORD

Oxford University Press, Walton Street, Oxford OX2 6DP

Oxford New York Toronto
Delhi Bombay Calcutta Madras Karachi
Petaling Jaya Singapore Hong Kong Tokyo
Nairobi Dar es Salaam Cape Town
Melbourne Auckland

and associated companies in
Berlin Ibadan

Oxford is a trade mark of Oxford University Press

© Oxford University Press 1991
Printed in Hong Kong

A CIP catalogue record for this book is available from the British
Library.

Acknowledgements
The Editor and Publisher wish to thank the following who have
kindly given permission for the use of copyright material:

Mary Dawson for Jack Frost © Mary Dawson; Eric Finney for Stop
calling me, snow © 1990 Eric Finney; John Foster for Ten White
Snowmen and The Brown Bear all © 1990 John Foster; Jean
Kenward for Frozen Stiff © 1990 Jean Kenward; Judith Nicholls for
Thin Ice! © 1990 Judith Nicholls; Jill Townsend for Snowball © 1990
Jill Townsend.

Although every effort has been made to contact the owners of
copyright material, a few have been impossible to trace, but if they
contact the Publisher correct acknowledgement will be made in
future editions.

4/92

Who saw the footprints in the snow?

Who saw the footprints in the snow?
Who came along and where did she go?

The farmer's wife has just been out
To scatter bits of bread about.

Who saw the footprints in the snow?
Who came along and where did he go?

One little sparrow was out today,
He ate some bread and hopped away.

Who saw the footprints in the snow?
Who came along and where did she go?

A pigeon ate some breadcrumbs too,
She walked around, then off she flew.

A cat crept up behind the hedge,
Then sprang on to the window ledge.

Who saw the footprints in the snow?
Who came along and where did she go?

A squirrel found the snow too deep,
So went off home to have some sleep.

On his horse, the farmers's son,
Went riding off to have some fun.

Anon

3

Stop calling me, snow

Stop calling me, snow,
I can't come just yet,
I've got ten sums to do
That the teacher just set.

So it's no good you flapping
Your downy white wings,
It's half an hour yet
Till the playtime bell rings.

Some kids will stay in,
But not me – no fear!
I'll dive straight for my wellies –
I can see them from here.

And I might build a snowman,
Or perhaps a snow queen,
Or I might just tread prints
Where nobody's been;

Then an igloo maybe,
With a tunnel to crawl,
Or perhaps I'll roll up
A monster snowball.

I'll stand in the whirl of your flakes
Till I'm dizzy,
But I can't come just yet –
I'm supposed to be busy . . .

There's this sum: 'Find
A half of a half.' I don't know . . .
I simply can't think . . .
Stop calling me, snow!

Eric Finney

Ten White Snowmen

Ten white snowmen standing in a line,
One toppled over, then there were nine.

Nine white snowmen standing up straight,
One lost his balance, then there were eight.

Eight white snowmen in a snowy heaven,
The wind blew one over, then there were seven.

Seven white snowmen with pipes made of sticks,
One slumped to the ground, then there were six.

Six white snowmen standing by the drive,
One got knocked down, then there were five.

Five white snowmen outside the front door,
An icicle fell on one, then there were four.

Four white snowmen standing by the tree,
One slipped and fell apart, then there were three.

Three white snowmen underneath the yew,
One crumbled overnight, then there were two.

Two white snowmen standing in the sun,
One melted right down, then there was one.

One white snowman standing all alone,
Vanished without a trace, then there were none.

John Foster

Thin Ice!

Andrew saw them skating
on the TV show;
thought that *he* should try it.
'Please Mum, let me go!'

'Now Andrew, don't go near the pond
or you will surely sink!
Wait till Saturday, we'll all
go to the skating rink.'

'Looks all right,' thought Andrew,
poked it with a stick.
'Anyone could skate on there –
it's clearly very thick!'

Slid along towards the sign
DANGER – ICE IS THIN!
Just had time to touch it . . .
then Andrew tumbled in.

Luckily a passer-by
heard him scream and shout;
grabbed the rope and life-buoy,
helped to pull him out.

On Saturday his Mum said
'Skating! Shall we go?'
Andrew paled and whispered fast
'No, I don't think so!'

Judith Nicholls

9

The Brown Bear

In winter,
When the cold winds blow,
When the land
Is covered with snow,
The brown bear sleeps.

In winter,
When the nights come soon,
When the land
Freezes beneath the moon
The brown bear dreams.

The brown bear
Dreams of summer heat,
Of berries,
Honey and nuts to eat.
The brown bear sighs.

The brown bear
Stirs, then digs down deep,
Safe and sound
In its winter sleep.
The brown bear dreams.

John Foster

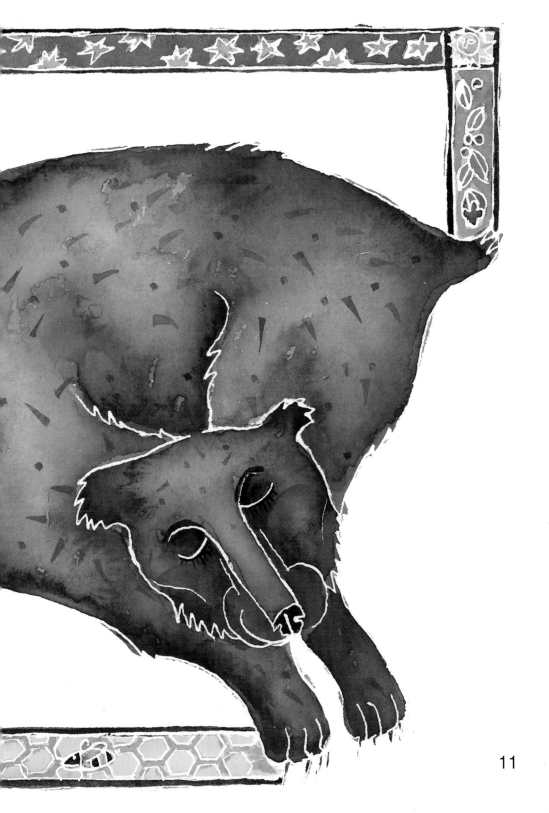

Jack Frost

Someone's painted patterns on the windows,
And I know who!
There are frosty ferns that sparkle
As the sun shines through.

Jack Frost, you nip our fingers!
Jack Frost, you nip our toes!
And we always know you're coming
When the north wind blows.

Someone's turned the water in the duck pond
To an icy sheet;
And now we've made some patterns
With our sliding feet.

Jack Frost, you nip our fingers!
Jack Frost, you nip our toes!
And we always know you're coming
when the north wind blows.

Mary Dawson

12

Frozen Stiff

Stiff as a battleship
prim as a pin
look at the washing
the frost is in!

Nighties, pyjamas
and petticoats too –
hard as the buckle
upon my shoe.

Punch them and pull them
they won't let go
of the long clothes line
for they love it so.

And however you tug them
they hold on tight
to the shivering pegs
with all their might,

As if they would cry
'Oh, leave us please!
We love to hang here
and freeze and freeze!'

Look at my trousers,
there's ice on the hem!
I shan't sit down
when I'm wearing them!

Jean Kenward   15

Snowball

Mine is a comet
whistling through space
towards a distant planet.
But the planet is a head
in a woolly hat
and my snowball misses it.

Jill Townsend

16